CH00839163

Lions, Whales
and Thrilling Tales

Lions, Whales
and Thrilling Tales

Alexa Tewkesbury and Steve Legg

CanaanPress

CanaanPress

Copyright © 2008 – Alexa Tewkesbury and Steve Legg

First printed in Great Britain in 2008 by
Canaan Press
PO Box 3070
Littlehampton
West Sussex
BN17 6WX
office@canaanpress.co.uk
www.canaanpress.co.uk

The book imprint of
Matt's Canaan Trust
www.mattscanaantrust.com

All rights reserved. No part of this publication may be reproduced,
stored in a retrieval system, or transmitted in any form or by any
means – for example, electronic, photocopy, recording – without
prior written permission of the publisher. The only exception is
brief quotations in printed reviews.

British Library Cataloguing in Publication Data
A record of this book is available from the British Library

ISBN: 978-0-9551816-4-1

Designed by Andy Ashdown
www.andyashdowndesign.co.uk

Illustrations by Bob Bond

Manufactured in Malta by Gutenberg Press Limited

"Just brilliant! These tales are punchy, modern, and fun, yet remain faithful to the Big Story from which they came. I loved them!"

BOB HARTMAN

"These stories bring Bible characters to life. They'll really help children understand what it must have felt like walking in those shoes."

DOUG HORLEY

"If you know a child who thinks the Bible is boring... then buy them this book!"

ISHMAEL

Contents

Introduction

Being human is a complicated business. We can be happy, sad, excited, bored, loving, hateful, creative, frustrated, ecstatic, miserable, generous, selfish, relaxed, uptight, funny or even outrageous – and that's just before breakfast! We're a mass of experiences, moods and emotions. It's what makes us who we are.

The people we read about in the Old Testament are no different. They had good times and bad times, just as we have, and they struggled with the same emotional highs and lows. Life certainly wasn't easy. God always stayed close to them, but when things went badly wrong, they must have wondered why He seemed to have disappeared.

Some of God's people tried to ignore Him. Some got angry. Some were full of fear. Others flatly refused to do as they were told. Still others showed amazing faith, and even when they had no idea what was going on, they kept on talking to God, never really doubting that He would hear them and answer their prayers. Then, through the complicated twists and turns of their lives, God taught them about His perfect love for them. He tested them, to their very limits sometimes, but only so that they would emerge stronger and draw even closer to Him.

This book retells some of those Old Testament adventures, but from the inside. Written from the point of view of the main characters themselves, the stories are meant to give a little insight into what it might have *felt* like to live through those events.

What must have gone through Daniel's mind as he was hurled head first into the pit of lions? What was it like for Joseph when he discovered his brothers had sold him for twenty pieces of silver? How hard must it have been for Hannah to have to leave her young son to grow up with Eli? What kind of fear must have gripped Jacob as he went to meet the brother he had betrayed so heartlessly? How angry must Jonah have been to try to run away from God? How satisfying was it for Ruth to see God finally put things right? What crazy mixture of happiness and disbelief must have filled Esther's head when King Xerxes made her his Queen? Our every day experiences may not be so extreme but, at times, the emotions we have to deal with can be just as powerful.

The more we can identify with God's people in the Bible, the more we'll be able to see that they were just like us: human beings. And just as God kept on loving them despite their anger, disobedience, doubts and fears, so He keeps on loving us. We all make mistakes. We all get things wrong. But God's love for each one of us is as strong as it ever was. As you read these very personal accounts, we hope you'll be able to hear God's heroes and heroines telling it like it is – or at least how it might have been for them.

Lions, Whales And Thrilling Tales

Dream On. . .

A lot of people look down their noses at shepherds, but actually it's not a bad way to earn a crust. All right, so you smell a bit by the end of the day, but who cares? It's the family business and I'm proud of it. When I was a kid I was always out in the fields helping the others with the animals. There are twelve of us. Eleven brothers and me. Well, one full brother and ten half brothers. And Dad, of course. Poor old Dad! We must have driven him nuts the way we were always falling out. You see, I was his favourite, so that made them all jealous. It was nothing I did, it's just that he was quite old when I was born and I think he must have seen me as a sort of bonus. Something he didn't expect. I'm not the youngest, though, that's Benjamin. He's my full brother because we had the same mum. Her name was Rachel and she was very special. Dad really loved her.

Maybe Dad did spoil me, I don't know, I wasn't very old. I was only seventeen when he called me in and gave me that amazing coat. The excitement was simmering in his voice when he said, "Joseph." (That's me.) "Come and see what I've got for you." And, wow, it really was some coat! He'd had it

specially made for me.

"Well?" he asked. "Do you like it?"

Like it? I loved it. My eyes must have been popping out of my head.

When my brothers saw me wearing it, their eyes popped out too – but not because they were thinking how fantastic I looked. It was more a case of, "Spoilt little brat, we're going to get you for this."

Not long after that, I started having some weird dreams. They showed me that one day my entire family would bow down to me – as if I was some kind of great leader or something. I should have known better than to say anything, but being a bit of a blabbermouth, out it all came. Naturally it went down like a lead balloon. Even Dad was annoyed. I had a funny feeling I was in trouble. What I didn't realise was quite how much.

It all started the day I went north of Jerusalem to Shecem. My brothers were meant to be grazing the animals there and Dad wanted me to check everything was all right. When I got there, I found out they'd left without me, and gone thirteen miles up the road to the ancient city of Dothan. So I went after them. I saw them in the distance and waved. They didn't wave back. I didn't expect them to, I suppose.

I didn't expect it when they grabbed my coat and threw me into a big hole in the ground either.

"Yeah, yeah, very funny, guys," I said. "Now how about helping me out?" They were all peering down at me, but their twisted up mouths and that "You're dead, Joseph!" expression blazing out of their eyes told me this was no joke.

I scanned the sides of the pit for something to hold on to so I could pull myself out, but there was nothing. I was stuck. Just me and the odd scorpion. I found out later they really would have killed me if it hadn't been for Reuben. He's the eldest. He was planning to rescue me or something. Now Reuben's a good shepherd but, as it turned out, rescuing people wasn't one of his strong points. He must have wandered off, because while he wasn't there my other rotten brothers sold me to a bunch of gypsies. The next thing I knew I was on the back of a camel on my way to Egypt.

That was a nightmare journey. I was scared witless but I couldn't get my brothers out of my head. All I remember thinking was, when Dad hears about this, you're going to be in so much trouble! Of course what I didn't realise then was that my brothers never let Dad know. They told him I was dead. Torn to pieces by wild animals. Can you believe it?

Dad did.

So there I was hundreds of miles from home, and not a friendly face in sight, but somehow, I knew I wasn't alone. God was with me. I couldn't see Him but He was there, which was just as well. When we finally arrived in Egypt, things started to look pretty bad.

"Come on, smile." A greasy, watery-eyed man winked at me. He had big, gappy teeth. "You're going up for sale. You'll make a lovely little slave, you will. And who knows? If you're really lucky, you might even get bought by someone nice."

I shuddered. A slave! So that's what my brothers had done. They'd sold me into slavery – for twenty pieces of silver. My mouth turned to sandpaper. I had visions of beatings and stale bread and being chucked outside at night to sleep with the pigs. "Get a grip," I told myself. "Maybe no-one'll buy you. Then they'll have to let you go."

But I did get bought, and quite quickly too, by this smart-looking man called Potiphar. He was something high up to do with Pharoah, the King of all Egypt. I was petrified but I thought, no, I'll work hard, do as I'm told and it'll be all right. So that's what I did... and amazingly it was. God made the best of everything. He never went away. He really looked after Potiphar's house and business. And me. Potiphar was over the moon, and he respected me because of what God was doing. In the end, he put me in charge of all his business, the whole lot. I wasn't a slave anymore, I was the one in control.

For a while after that, life was pretty good, and I suppose it would have stayed that way if it hadn't been for one tiny problem – Potiphar's wife.

Though I say it myself, I was a bit of a good-looker. I mean, I knew she liked me, she was always hanging around. I could see her watching me. It was all, "Joseph, what do you think of my hair like this?" and, "Do me a favour, Joseph, tell me how I look in this robe." I was a bit slow on the uptake in those days so I wasn't sure what was going on. In the end she had to tell me. She didn't just like me, she really fancied me. Potiphar's wife fancied me! I almost laughed in her face, she must have been mental. Potiphar was my boss. He trusted me. What did she expect me to do? Whatever it was I didn't do it. I couldn't betray him like that and I told her so. She got really stroppy and told Potiphar a string of lies about me. I was supposed to have attacked her or something. I told him none of it was true but he was so angry he didn't believe a word I said, and had me thrown into jail. Unbelievable. I was locked up because some woman had a massive crush on me.

It was pretty grim in that prison I can tell you, but God never left me, not once. After a bit, the governor even started to get quite friendly. He must have trusted me, too, because one day he put me in charge of all the other prisoners. That was God's doing.

There were all sorts of characters shut away in that prison and did they have some tales to tell. A couple of them used to work for Pharoah, himself, until they got on the wrong side of him and he locked them up. They were usually quite a cocky pair, but one morning I noticed them looking a bit down.

"Why the long faces?" I asked.

"Oh, it's nothing," one of them said. But he looked uncomfortable so I knew something was up.

"Come on, out with it," I persisted. "Been winding up the governor again?"

"No, no, it's nothing like that." The man hesitated and glanced at his mate. Then he told me.

"I mean it's daft, really, it's just... we've both had these weird dreams. And I know they mean something, but I'm not sure what. We're scared, see? What if it's something bad?"

Weird dreams were something I knew all about. I knew God could help me explain them too, so I said, "Well, let's not panic. Sit down and tell me about them and God'll help me work out what's going on."

Pharoah's butler told me *his* dream first.

"I saw a vine growing," he said awkwardly, as if he didn't want to say it at all. "It had three branches and they were covered in grapes. I picked them, squeezed out the juice into Pharoah's cup and gave it to him."

"Is that it?" I could feel a broad grin spreading across my face. I knew straight away what it meant.

"Things are looking up," I told him, clapping a hand on his shoulder. "You've got another three days in here, then Pharoah's going to let you out and give you your job back. You'll be serving his wine again by the end of the week."

That butler's face was a picture. I've never seen anyone look so relieved.

"Do me a favour, though," I went on. "When you get out, have a quiet word with His Majesty and see if you can get me out too."

He promised he would.

Then I listened to Pharoah's baker. Hearing his friend's good news, he was already looking a lot happier. In *his* dream he told me he was carrying three baskets on his head. They were packed with freshly baked bread and pastries for Pharoah, but the birds were eating them all. He finished speaking and waited expectantly.

A shiver shot through me. The baker stared intently into my face, but as he watched me, his smile vanished.

"Well?" He spoke in barely a whisper.

How could I tell him?

"You're not going to like this," I said at last. I had a dry mouth and my tongue felt like a piece of old leather.

"Pharoah plans to let you out in three days too, but you're not getting your job back." This was the tough bit. "I'm afraid he's going to hang you."

There was a horrible silence.

The three days came and went and the dreams came true. I never heard another thing from that butler though, at least not for a long time. Once he was out he forgot all about me. That was it, then. I'd be locked up for ever. What a grim little victory my brothers had won.

The Big Time

MORE ABOUT JOSEPH FROM THE BOOK OF GENESIS,
CHAPTERS 41–47

Funny how things happen when you least expect them. It
was two years since Pharoah's butler had promised to help
get me out of prison. Small wonder I'd given up on him.
There were days when I felt like giving up on everything.

Then, out of the blue, I heard that Pharoah had started
having dreams and was asking everywhere for someone to
explain them, but no-one could. That's when the butler
remembered me and I got a call to the palace.

I'd been in prison so long I must have looked disgusting. I
couldn't face the king like that, so I was allowed a quick
change and a shave before I saw him. You have no idea how
good that felt. And then there I was, standing in front of
Pharoah, the ruler of all Egypt. I was really scared. I told him
I could only explain dreams because God showed me their
meaning, but what if he didn't like what he heard? What if it
was terrible news like the baker's? I wanted the ground to
swallow me up, but it didn't.

"I've had two dreams," Pharoah began. "In the first, I was

standing by the River Nile when seven big, fat cows climbed out of the water and started eating the grass. Then, suddenly seven more cows followed them up the bank, but they were skinny, bony-looking things and they didn't want the grass. Instead they ate up the fat cows right there in front of me. In the second I saw seven shoots of corn growing out of one stalk. They were all ripe and healthy. Then another stalk shot up, again with seven shoots, but these were dry and pathetic-looking, and they ate the good stuff."

As Pharoah finished speaking I felt so relieved I could have kissed him! I didn't have to tell him he was about to be chucked off his throne or murdered in his bed.
"God's letting you know what's going to happen," I said chirpily. "The next seven years will be really good for Egypt. There'll be bumper harvests and more food than you'll know what to do with. But the seven years after that will be disastrous. There's going to be a terrible famine. The crops won't grow and a lot of people will go very hungry. What you need to do is make sure enough grain gets stored away while there's plenty, so that everyone will have food in the years when there isn't any."

Pharoah was delighted, not because there were hard times ahead but because now he could plan for them. And guess what? He said he could see I was a man of God and he wanted me to be the one in charge – and not just of food storage. He asked me to look after the affairs of the whole country. God certainly likes to keep me on my toes. I mean, who'd have thought it? One minute I was a prisoner, the next I was Governor of Egypt. Pharoah even gave me his own ring to wear, a gold chain to put round my neck and a chariot to ride in. I almost had to pinch myself to make sure it wasn't *me* who was dreaming.

It wasn't an easy life, mind you, those first seven years were hard work. There was plenty to do, and it was down to me to make sure that all the farmers gave up a chunk of their harvests for storage. They probably thought I was potty. But God knew what He was doing. When the seven bad years began Pharoah could still feed his people. And it wasn't just Egypt that was in trouble. There was famine in other countries too. Foreigners started pouring in from everywhere and I could sort them all out with food.

Then one day, I got the shock of my life.

I was told a group of ten lads from Canaan were here to buy grain. I never gave it a thought, just called them in. And there they were. My brothers. Not Benjamin, but all the others. They didn't recognise me, but I knew *them*. My jaw must have hit the floor, and as I stood there gawping, the strangest thing happened. They all bowed down to me... and I remembered my dream.

I couldn't think straight, so I said the first thing that came
into my head.

"You haven't come here to buy food. Look at you! You're
spies! You're here to try and dig up state secrets."

They were horrified. I watched them squirm.

"No, no, you don't understand," they stammered, "we're just
a family. Our dad's at home with our youngest brother. We
need food, that's all."

But I wasn't having it. I needed time to think. After all those
years I wanted to know if they were truly sorry for what
they'd done. I wanted to see dad and I wanted to see
Benjamin, but I couldn't just carry on as though nothing had
happened. So I had them locked up – for three days. Well, it
was nothing, was it, compared to what they'd done to me.
Then I went to see them.

"If you're not spies, prove it," I demanded. "*You're* going to
stay here," and I pointed to Simeon. "The rest of you can go
home with food for your families, but the next time you
come, you bring your youngest brother. If you don't, I'll
know you've been telling me a pack of lies." I jerked my head
towards Simeon adding, "And you won't get this one back." I
amazed myself. I was really tough.

Then I ordered my brothers' sacks to be filled with grain, and
made sure the money they'd paid was put in with it. When

they found it, I knew they'd be worried. Maybe I did want to rattle them a bit, but they were still my family. I didn't want their money. As far as I was concerned, they could have the food as a present.

When they'd gone, I tried to stop thinking about them. I *wanted* to stop thinking about them. But I couldn't. Every night when I went to bed I thought, maybe they'll come back tomorrow, and every morning when I woke up I'd wonder if this was the day they'd arrive. Months went by with not a word, no news, no message, nothing. Perhaps it was my fault. Maybe I'd overdone it and scared them off. I didn't want to believe they'd dump Simeon like they'd dumped me, but it looked as though they had. And I felt dumped all over again.

Then one day when I'd almost given up, they did come back. They'd run out of food again. And just as I'd ordered them, they'd brought Benjamin. I couldn't help staring. He looked so grown up I hardly recognised him. He certainly didn't know me. Whatever had it cost Dad to let him go? I could feel myself getting all choked up.

"Let's eat together back at my place," I blurted out, and sent them off to my house where the servants did us a wonderful, slap-up meal. I had Simeon brought over too, and we all had a really good time together. The servants heaped Benjamin's plate with food. I told them to give him five times as much as everyone else. He looked as if he needed feeding up. Of course, my brothers couldn't work out what was going on. They were convinced they were in trouble because it looked as if they hadn't paid for their last lot of grain. I was dying to tell them who I was, but, no, not yet. I needed to wait just a little while longer.

They all stayed the night and the next morning the servants loaded them up with grain again, and put their money back in their sacks, just like before. This time, though, I had a plan. If my brothers were really sorry, I was going to find out. I told a servant to hide one of my best silver wine cups in Benjamin's sack when he wasn't looking. Then I saw them all off on their donkeys and they began their journey home. They wouldn't have got far when I sent some of my men after them to accuse them of stealing the cup. Of course, they denied it, and they must have been pretty shaken up when there it was in Benjamin's sack. My men brought them all back here.
"What a bunch of low-lifes!" I said. "Haven't I given you enough, so now you're stealing from me as well?"

I watched their faces. They looked so sad. Defeated somehow. More than that, I could see how guilty they were feeling. Not about the cup. They knew God could see the wrong they'd done me. I reckon they thought they were being punished. I wanted to shout out, "It's me, it's Joseph!" but I didn't. I had a plan and I was going to see it through. So instead I said, "This cup was found in one of your sacks. Whoever that sack belongs to, you're staying here. You're going to be my slave."

I waited. I think I was holding my breath. Would they say, "All right", turn their backs on Benjamin, walk away? If they did I'd know they couldn't care less. But suddenly they were all shaking their heads. They looked desperate, but they knew what had to be done. It was Judah who started pleading with me.

"You can't do this," he said, "you can't keep him." I thought he was going to burst into tears. I was on the point of it myself!

"Please," he went on, "I promised I'd take Benjamin home again. Our dad will go to pieces if we go back without him. He's already lost one son. Losing another, well, it'll kill him. *I'll* stay. *I'll* be your slave. Just, please, let Benjamin go."

I was shaking. I'd found out it was Judah's idea to sell me into slavery in the first place, and now here he was, offering to give up his freedom for Benjamin. I don't know what I felt – pleased, amazed, relieved? Whatever it was, I had to send the servants out. I couldn't let them see me crying. My brothers were sorry. They really were.

"It's all right," I managed to say. It was a struggle to speak.
"It's me. Joseph!"

Of course, hearing that scared them to death. By the horrified looks on their faces, they must have thought I was going to get my own back in some seriously nasty way.

"No, no," I spluttered, "I'm not going to hurt you. I know you're sorry and I can see it had to be this way. It was God who sent me here. This is where He wanted me to be. Whatever I've been through, it was all part of His plan. You see, we've still got five more years of bad harvests to get through and a lot of people are going to die. But because God's put me here, I can save you. I can save our whole family."

Those brothers of mine couldn't believe what they were hearing. I told them to go back to Canaan, get everyone packed up to move, then come here and I'd settle them all into a little place called Goshen in the north of Egypt. It was perfect for grazing and farming and they'd be safe there with enough food to last until the bad times were over.

"Are you serious?" They just couldn't make me out. "You really want us here after everything we've done to you?"

"Come on," I said, "you know what family stuff's like. Probably happens all the time!"

So that's how it turned out. There'd come a time when they'd return to Canaan, but for now they left it behind and moved

here to Egypt, wives, children, servants, everyone. They even brought the animals.

I can't describe what it was like seeing my dad after all those years. We must have hugged and talked for hours. And when I took him to meet the king, I think he was really proud. As for being a family again, well, it was better than any dream.

LIONS, WHALES AND THRILLING TALES

Happily Ever After

THE BOOK OF RUTH

"I hate moving house!" Naomi must have said that a hundred times as she stomped about packing up the family possessions ready for their journey to Moab. She loved their little home in Bethlehem, so when her husband, Elimelech, said they'd have to leave, I can imagine her throwing a bit of a wobbly. But back then it was becoming impossible to stay. There was a famine. People were starving and the ground was too dried up to give them any food. Knowing Naomi, I bet she wanted to dig in her heels and say, "Let's just give it another couple of months." But she knew Elimelech was right and, apart from anything else, they had their two sons to think of. So it was decided. They'd have to emigrate.

Moab was fifty miles away from Bethlehem, across the River Jordan on the other side of the Dead Sea. The famine hadn't reached that far so they'd be safe there. They could start a new life. Only after they arrived, things didn't quite go according to plan. Elimelech died. Well, poor Naomi. Her boys were wonderful, Mahlon and Kilion, but she still must have felt so alone.

Of course, she was over the moon when they got married because suddenly her family got bigger again. She had two daughters-in-law, Orpah, and me, Ruth – and *that* got her thinking about grandchildren. She was so excited, I'm surprised she didn't start making baby clothes right there and then.

It's a good job she didn't, though, because the grandchildren never came. Just as life was beginning to pick up after she'd lost her husband, her two sons died as well. And there we were, three lonely widows.

We tried to make a go of things after that, but I think ten years in Moab was more than enough for Naomi. She couldn't settle, and when news finally came through from Bethlehem that God had brought an end to the famine, all she wanted to do was go back home.

Orpah wasn't happy.
"I don't want to leave here," she complained to me miserably. "*This* is our home, not Bethlehem."
"I know," I said, "but what can we do? Naomi's getting old. We can't let her go on her own, we're all she's got."

So we packed up and moved out of Moab.

As we set off, Naomi was unusually quiet. I tried to get some chat going, you know, cheer us all up a bit, but it was a waste

of time. Then, suddenly, Naomi stopped dead.

"It's no good," she said abruptly, "you'll have to go back."

I felt a bit annoyed, I couldn't help it.

"What for?" I asked. "Have we forgotten something?"

"Don't be daft," Naomi snapped. "You just can't come with me, that's all."

I hadn't a clue what she was on about, and from the look on Orpah's face, neither had she.

Naomi shook her head impatiently. "I can't let you leave Moab. I know how bad it feels to be forced to leave your home." She sounded harsh but she wasn't. The grief that darkened her eyes in their pale, lined sockets gave her away. "Go on, go back." She motioned with her hand. "And may God bless you and help you find new husbands to take care of you."

"But we've already decided to come with you," said Orpah, "we've said goodbye and everything."

Naomi turned away. She could be so stubborn when she wanted to be.

"Coming with me won't find you a husband," she answered. "Go on home and get on with your life."

Suddenly we were all hugging and saying this gut-wrenching goodbye. Then Orpah turned and headed back for Moab.

Naomi looked at me. We both had tears streaming down our

cheeks, but she brushed hers away impatiently.

"Well," she said, "off you go. Orpah's gone, if you're quick you'll catch up with her."

But I could be stubborn too. I wasn't going to leave Naomi to grow old on her own. So I said quietly, "No, I'm coming with you. If Bethlehem's good enough for you, it's good enough for me. I'm sure I'll fit in. And I'll learn about this God you talk about and get to know Him too. No arguments. That's it."
I wasn't usually so blunt and Naomi looked a bit surprised. But she didn't say a word. She just took my hand and gave it a squeeze, and we set off, the two of us, on our way again.

As much as she didn't want to stay in Moab, it must have been desperately hard for Naomi being back in Bethlehem. I really felt for her. Her friends were all thrilled to see her and they gave her a wonderful welcome. But the last time she was there she had a husband and a family. Now she only had me.

I did my best for her though. It was April when we arrived and the barley harvest was just beginning. We had no money, but I told her I'd go out into the fields and pick up the grain the harvesters left behind so at least we'd have something to eat.

Bringing in the harvest was hard graft. You needed a good team of workers, the men to cut the ripe, standing grain with their razor sharp sickles, and the women to follow behind

tying it into sheaves. Then poor people like me would do the gleaning, which meant crawling along on our hands and knees picking up the stalks of grain that had been dropped and left behind. The law said the poor were allowed to do that. I was filthy by the end of each day.

I began working in a field that belonged to a man called Boaz. I could tell he was the owner from the minute he walked through the gate. He started talking to some of the workers and they were looking at me. I felt all nervous. I mean, there I was, a foreigner in *his* field picking up *his* left-over barley. I tried telling myself, "Come on, you're not doing anything wrong." But then, out of the corner of my eye, I saw him making his way towards me. I thought, perfect, now I'm in for it.

I was all ready to leap in and defend myself, but Boaz got there first.

"It's all right," he said gently. He must have seen I was panicking. "You're welcome to carry on working here with my harvesters. Stay with them, I've told them to leave you alone. They've got some water jars filled over there. When you're thirsty go and help yourself."

I couldn't believe what I was hearing. I thought this must be his idea of a joke and any minute I'd be out on my ear.

"Why would you do this for me?" I asked. "I'm not even from round here."

"I know who you are, though," Boaz answered, "and I know how good you've been to Naomi. May God reward you for all you've done."
I could hardly carry on working I was trembling so much. I think gob-smacked is the word. God was certainly with me that day.

And there was more. When the workers stopped for something to eat, Boaz asked me to join them all and share some bread and roasted grain. He gave me so much there was enough left over to take home to Naomi, along with all the barley I'd collected. You should have seen her face when I told her whose field I'd been working in.
"Boaz!" she shrieked excitedly. "Are you sure it's Boaz?"
"Yes, so what?" I was mystified.
"God hasn't forgotten us," she smiled. "Boaz is a relative of Elimelech. He's a part of our family. You do as he says and stay with his harvesters. You'll be safe with them."

I didn't care whether Boaz was family or not. He'd been kind to us, that's all that mattered, and I was able to carry on gathering food until the harvest was over.

But Naomi hadn't told me the full story. It was a while after that before she explained to me that, in Israel, when a man died his nearest relation was responsible for looking after the rest of the family. It was the law.

"You need a husband," Naomi said, "someone who'll take care of you. Boaz is a good man. You'll have to go a long way to do better than him."

"Oh, Mum!" I could feel myself blushing. But Naomi wasn't about to let an opportunity like this slip by. She had it all worked out.

"Boaz will be down at the threshing-floor tonight, keeping an eye on his barley," Naomi began, her face bright with anticipation. "Now, you're to have a good wash, put on your best clothes and get yourself down there. Oh, and spray yourself with something nice. You know what men are like when they catch a whiff of perfume. And remember, you're entitled to be his wife. Explain it to him, see what he says." Then she added, "This is just between the three of us, mind. Don't you tell anyone."

I was hardly likely to do that. It was embarrassing enough having to talk to Boaz without letting someone else in on it. It all seemed so forward. I mean, supposing he took one look at me and said, "Sorry, love, but I don't think so." I'd never be able to look him in the face again. But there was no getting out of it. Naomi's mind was made up and that was that. As I crept out to the threshing-floor through the blackness of the night, I could have died a hundred times over.

"Of course I'll marry you. It would be an honour." I heard

Boaz say the words but I didn't dare believe he meant them.

"What?" My voice was little more than a squeak.

"I'll marry you," he repeated. "Why wouldn't I? Everyone knows what a good woman you are."

I stood there gaping at him.

"There is just one problem," he went on.

Oh, here we go, I thought, I knew it was too good to be true.

"I'm not your only family," he said. "You have a relation whose closer to you than I am. I can't marry you without agreeing it with him first."

When I got home I found Naomi pacing the floor in agitation.

"Well?" she demanded, her inquisitive eyes eagerly searching my face. When I told her what Boaz had said, she clapped her hands together gleefully.

"We'll know soon enough," she said. "Boaz isn't a man to let things rest till they're sorted."

She was right. Boaz didn't waste any time. He got together ten witnesses and met this other relative of ours at the town gate, which was where important meetings were held and business done. He told the man that Elimelech's property was up for sale and that with ownership of that property went responsibility for his widow, Naomi, and his daughter-in-law, Ruth. But the man already had land and a family, and didn't want to take on any more.

So it was decided. In front of all those witnesses, Boaz announced that he was going to marry me. Me! There was plenty to gossip about in Bethlehem that day, I can tell you.

What a wedding we had. Naomi was positively glowing, but that was nothing to the radiance in her face the day I gave birth to my little boy. We called him Obed and he was a proper little smasher. Naomi had a grandchild at last. After everything she'd been through God found a way to put it all right.

And me? I often think about my first meeting with Boaz in his field when he asked God to reward me. He couldn't have had any idea God would use him to answer his own prayer. It didn't matter though. God knew.

Lions, Whales And Thrilling Tales

Twin Trouble

JACOB'S STORY FROM THE BOOK OF GENESIS,
CHAPTERS 25 AND 27–29

Squirm, wriggle, thump, bump. That's what Mum said it was
like when my brother and I were growing together inside her.
Even before we were born we didn't give her a minute's peace.
In the end she asked God, "What in the world is going on in
there?"

"You're carrying twin boys," He told her, "and they will
eventually become the fathers of two nations. Their
descendants will form two separate peoples, two nationalities.
And as they grow up, the older brother will serve the younger."

If that doesn't sound like a recipe for conflict, I don't know
what does. Of course it shouldn't have been that way. If we'd
trusted God and allowed His plans to unfold, we could have
saved ourselves so much grief. But we didn't. We interfered.
And when you interfere with God's plan, there's always a
price to pay.

Our parents, Isaac and Rebekah, named my brother Esau and
me Jacob. Esau was the older twin. He was born first, but
only just. When I popped out close behind him, I was

hanging on to his heel. Mum was tickled pink. She'd been married to Isaac for twenty years and had waited all that time for a baby. Then two came along at once.

As twin brothers go, we couldn't have been more different. We didn't look alike for a start. Esau was a hairy little chap from birth, but my skin was quite smooth and bare. Esau was the outdoor type and a great hunter. He brought home no end of wild animals for cooking up in stews which Dad loved. I think Dad had a real soft spot for him. But me, I was a home-loving boy and I spent a lot of time with Mum. I suppose that's why I was her favourite.

Whatever our differences may have been, I did a bad thing to Esau. As Mum and Dad's older son, the firstborn, he was entitled to be head of the family when Dad died and to inherit twice as much of the family property as I would. It was his birthright. But I wanted it. After all, God had told Mum that her older son would serve the younger and, if I was meant to be greater than him, that birthright ought to be mine. So one day, when Esau came home from a long day's hunting absolutely starving, I made sure I got it.

I'd been cooking, and, when Esau smelt the stew simmering in the pot, he couldn't wait to tuck into a bowlful.

"Serve it up then," he demanded, "I haven't eaten for hours."

I stirred the pot slowly as the greed gleamed in Esau's eyes.
The delicious smell was obviously driving him mad.

"Come on," he snapped irritably, "I'm dying of hunger here."

I blew on a ladle of hot stew to cool it and tasted a mouthful.
It was very good.

Esau was stunned.
"Have you gone deaf or something?" He was fast losing his
temper. "I said I'm famished, now give me some stew."
I didn't look at him, just stirred the pot casually and replied,
"I'll give you some stew if you agree to sell me your
birthright."
"Are you mad?" Esau exploded. "I just want some food."
"And you can have some," I answered coolly, "as much as you
can eat. Just sell me your birthright first."

Esau's stomach was beginning to get the better of him. He
gazed longingly down into the cooking pot, then shook his
head impatiently.
"Oh, have it," he muttered. "It's no good to me anyway. I shall
be dead from starvation in a minute."

He picked up a bowl and held it out. I don't think he was
taking me seriously.

"Swear it," I said.

"What?" He stared at me incredulously, but I said nothing. "All right, all right, I swear it," he spluttered. "Now let me eat before I fall over!"

And that was that. Esau had traded his birthright for a bowl of stew, and my long struggle with God had begun.

It wasn't just Esau and me who put the family to shame. Mum and Dad had a hand in it too, and between the four of us we did a pretty good job of screwing things up for good.

As Dad got old he started to go blind, and with the world around him sinking into darkness he couldn't help wondering how much longer he had to live. One day Mum came running to find me. She looked so disturbed I thought something terrible must have happened, but she grasped my hands excitedly.

"Your father's been talking to Esau. He wants to give him his blessing before he dies. He's told Esau to go hunting out in the hills and bring back something tasty for a stew. Then, when your father has eaten, he'll give the blessing."

I frowned. "Esau's not going along with it, is he?" He couldn't. He'd sold his birthright to me. He'd sworn an oath. That special blessing wasn't his to receive.

"Yes, he is," Mum nodded vigorously. "He's just set off with all his gear. That's why we've got to get a shift on. *You* should be the one getting that blessing. Now here's what we're going to do. You nip out and bring me two young goats from the herd. Then I'll cook up a thick, spicy stew for your dad, something with a bit of bite. When it's ready you can take it to him. You can pretend to be Esau. The poor man's nearly blind. If you wear Esau's clothes, he'll never know the difference."

"What about my skin?" I asked. "I'm not hairy like Esau. If Dad touches me, he'll know it's a trick."

"I've already thought of that. We'll cover your hands and neck with goatskin. That'll be good and rough."

I didn't have time to stop and think, I just did as Mum said. Dad shouldn't be giving the blessing to Esau. It was mine. It's what God had planned before we were even born – the older would serve the younger. But that was the moment we should have turned to God for help.

Only we didn't. We didn't talk to Him at all.

Dressed in Esau's best clothes and with the goatskin covering my hands and neck, I picked up the freshly-prepared food and took it to Dad. If I was afraid at all, it wasn't of God. It was because I thought that, in spite of his blindness, Dad would see through me. He would know I was trying to trick him. Then, instead of blessing me, he would curse me.

Dad was sitting in his usual spot, quietly waiting. I took a deep breath and marched up to him.

"Here we are then," I said as boldly as I could. "You wait till you taste this."
Dad's face lit up. "Is that really you, Esau?" he asked. "You sound just like Jacob."

I laid the food in his lap. As I did so, he reached out and touched my hands. I froze while his fingers explored the goat hair.

"Of course it's me," I lied.

Dad smiled and nodded. "Esau's hands," he murmured. "Now I must eat, then I can give you my blessing."

He believed me. He enjoyed his meal and suspected nothing. Then he prayed over me that God would bless me with a life of power and plenty. And I stood there with my eyes wide open and deceived my father.

When Esau came home, he began to make a stew for Dad. I could hear him whistling cheerfully. He was obviously excited about receiving his blessing. I wondered if it crossed

his mind that he was breaking the promise he'd made when he sold me his birthright. Whether it did or not, I knew he'd be furious when he found out what I'd done.

"Best keep out of his way," Mum said, still glowing because Dad had blessed her favourite.

That turned out to be the best advice she could have given me. I don't think either of us realised what a torrent of rage was about to be let loose. Esau took Dad his steaming bowl of stew and placed it proudly in his lap. From my hiding place I could hear them talking, but the sound was muffled and I couldn't make out the words – until Esau began to shout and rave.

"But that was *my* blessing. Jacob's already stolen my birthright. How could you give him my blessing too?"
"He deceived me," Dad cried. "I thought he was you."
"Then bless me too," Esau pleaded. "Come on, there must be something for me."
"There's nothing." Dad's voice sounded tired and hollow. "I only have one blessing to give and your brother has taken it."

There was silence for a moment. Then I heard Esau begin to cry. I could sense his strong, powerful body shuddering as he sobbed. I'd done that to him. And I felt chilled to my heart.

From that moment life took a dive. Our family was shattered. Mum and Dad's marriage was wrecked and, as for Esau, his anger towards me quickly turned to hate. I was in big trouble.

Mum came to me soon afterwards, looking pale and frightened. "You've got to get out of here," she whispered. "Esau's planning to kill you. I don't know when or how, you must just go now."
I felt my stomach sinking fast.
"I want you to go and stay with my brother, Laban, in Padden-Aram," she went on quickly. "He'll look after you. Esau won't stay angry for ever. When he's calmed down I'll let you know and you can come home."
"I don't want to leave you, Mum," I blurted out.
She took my face in her hands, such sadness swimming in the dark pools of her eyes. "I'm sorry, Jacob," she murmured. "We have no choice. I'll sort it with your dad."

Mum did sort it. She told Dad she hated the thought that I'd end up having to marry a local girl. She couldn't stand any of them. So Dad told me to go to Padden-Aram to stay with Mum's family and to choose a wife from among my Uncle Laban's daughters – which is exactly what Mum wanted him to say.

The journey north to Padden-Aram was long and, as the sun

set on that miserable day, I lay down to rest. All I could think of was Mum. What a mess we'd made. Leaving her was the hardest thing I'd ever done. I found a stone and put it under my head as a pillow, but I thought I'd never get to sleep. My feet were too cold.

How far into the night I lay awake I've no idea. When at last I dozed off, I had the strangest dream. I saw an enormous staircase reaching from the ground right up into heaven. There were angels moving up and down the steps, and right at the very top stood God, and He began to talk to me.

"I am the Lord," He said. "This land where you have made your bed I will give to you and your descendants. There will be many of them and they will spread to the north, south, east and west. I am with you to care for you wherever you go. And I will lead you back to this land. This is my promise."

When I woke up and looked around me, nothing had changed, yet everything was different. God had spoken to me. Although I'd deceived my family, He still loved me. He'd visited me here. I thought I must be at the gate of heaven. I had to mark the spot somehow. So I took the stone I'd rested my head on and stood it upright in the dust. Then I poured a little oil onto it (it was all I could think of to make it special) and decided to call the place Bethel, which means "House of God". And before I moved on I prayed. God had made me a promise, so I made one to Him.

"If you will stay with me," I said, "if you will take care of me on this journey and one day return me safely to my family, you will be my Lord and my God."

Then I set off again to find my Uncle Laban. I must have trudged for miles over the hard, dusty ground. I was exhausted. The only thing keeping me going was the fact that I knew I couldn't go back. But one day, when I felt I couldn't carry on much longer, I happened to spot a group of shepherds near a well where they'd brought their sheep for water. I asked about Laban and they knew him. It was the best news I'd had since my dream.

"And if you're looking for him," one of them went on, "you're in luck. There's his daughter, Rachel."

A girl was walking towards the well followed by a huddle of sheep. I ran to meet her and, when I explained who I was, she said excitedly, "Wait till I tell Dad." It was such a relief to be with family again that I couldn't help giving her a big kiss. And when I met Uncle Laban, he welcomed me into his home like a long-lost son.

TWIN TROUBLE

Israel

MORE ABOUT JACOB FROM THE BOOK OF GENESIS, CHAPTERS 29–33

Living with my Uncle Laban was certainly a lot different to what I'd been used to but, even though I missed home, in a way I quite liked it. Things were made even better by Rachel. She was the younger of Laban's two daughters. The older one was Leah. I got on with them both, but there was just something about Rachel. After only a few weeks I was really falling for her.

That first month I was quite happy being part of the family and working for Laban. Then one day he said to me, "This is no good. Just because you're my nephew doesn't mean I shouldn't be paying you for all your hard work. What shall we make your wages?"

I hesitated. There was only one thing I wanted and it wasn't money. But would Laban consider it?

"What if I work for you for nothing for seven years?" I suggested. "In return, will you let me marry Rachel?"

There was silence. Laban's eyes narrowed as he eyed me up and down. That's it, I thought, I've blown it. But suddenly his face spread into a broad grin.

"Sounds fair to me," he answered, clapping me on the back. "In seven years, she's yours."

Now seven years might sound a long time but I loved Rachel so much they seemed to pass in a flash. And what a prize waited for me at the end. When the wedding day finally arrived, Laban threw a huge party to celebrate. I was so excited I didn't know where to put myself. It never occurred to me he planned to cheat me of my bride. But cheat me he did. He gave me the wrong daughter. I'd worked for him for seven years and he gave me Leah instead of Rachel.

"How could you do this to me?" As I stared at him, I could hardly speak. "After all I've done for you."

"Don't look so down," Laban smirked. He seemed to think it was all a big joke. "It's the custom in my country for the older daughter to marry before the younger one. Now that you've married Leah, you're welcome to marry Rachel as well. But afterwards, you must work for me for another seven years."

I suppose I wasn't really in a position to condemn him. After all, he was doing no worse to me than I'd done to Esau, for just as I'd betrayed my twin brother, Laban had betrayed me.

There was nothing I could do. If I didn't agree, I'd lose Rachel. And although I'd have to work without wages for another seven years, at least this time I'd have her with me as my wife. The trouble was that now Leah was my wife too and home wasn't a happy place. I couldn't love Leah, not the way I loved Rachel, and Leah knew it. To make matters worse,

God blessed Leah with lots of children – she gave me six sons and a daughter – while poor Rachel had none. That caused some arguments, I can tell you.

Then, finally, Rachel did have a baby, a little boy she called Joseph. What a day that was! I don't suppose it helped Leah, but I was thrilled to bits. That's when I began thinking about home. I'd worked for Laban for long enough. It was time to move on. I had my own family to think of and I wanted to take them back where I came from.

I knew persuading Laban to let me go wouldn't be easy. God had blessed my work and Laban had done really well since I'd been there. Now he was a rich man.
"Don't leave," he said to me, grasping my shoulders. "I know I've done well because God's been with you. Let's not be hasty, eh? If you stay on with me, I'll pay you anything you ask. What do you say?"

Now there was an offer I couldn't refuse. I didn't want money though. If Laban wanted me to stay that badly, he could pay me in animals. I asked for all the spotted and speckled sheep and goats from the herds, and for the dark coloured lambs.
"Done!" he cried rubbing his hands.

But good as Laban was at striking bargains, he was even

better at not keeping to them. As he spoke, he had a gleam in his eye that should have put me on my guard. Before I knew it, that crafty old man had cheated me again. He took all the animals I'd asked for and gave them to his sons to look after so that when I came to sort them from the herd, they were nowhere to be found. God helped me, though. I kept to my side of the agreement and looked after Laban's flocks. When they produced young, they were speckled and spotted and I could separate them from the other animals and keep them for myself and my family. After a time I made lots of money. But the better things went for me in business, the more unpopular I became with my relations. Laban was far less friendly, and his sons practically accused me of stealing from him. Then God told me it was definitely time to go home.

"Pack up everything you can and bring the children," I said to Rachel and Leah. "We're leaving." I said nothing to Laban. If he knew I was planning to take my family and the herds of animals I'd earned away from him, he'd never let us go. So when he was away shearing his sheep, we made our escape across the River Euphrates and headed off for my father Isaac's home in Canaan.

It was three days before Laban discovered we'd gone. Then he came after us.

We kept the pace up as much as we could, but travelling with children and livestock was bound to slow us down. A week or so later I caught sight of a dark group of figures on the horizon. I knew it was Laban.

"Come on," I urged, "we've got to keep moving."

"No," sighed Rachel. "The children are exhausted, the animals too. It's no good, we'll have to stop and make camp. At least we're in amongst the hills now, they could easily lose sight of us here. They might even give up and go home."

But Laban didn't give up. With his bunch of cronies tagging along behind, he tracked us down. There was nothing for it but to stand up and face him.

"Why have you done this?" he demanded. "I deserved the chance to say goodbye to my family. I could have given you a good send off, but oh no, you had to sneak away. You had to steal my daughters, my grandchildren, my animals." He paused, then in a quiet voice added, "God spoke to me in a dream last night and warned me not to do you any harm. If He hadn't, I could really hurt you now."

I thought I'd be afraid but I wasn't. What I felt was anger, fury. I'd been used for long enough.

"If I'd come to you to say goodbye, you'd never have let me go," I shouted back. "You wouldn't have let me leave with your daughters. I've worked for you for twenty years – fourteen years in exchange for your daughters and six more to build up some livestock for myself. I've been completely honest with you and all you've done is try to cheat me. If I hadn't had God on my side, you'd have sent me packing with nothing. But God *is* with me, and He's let you know you're not getting away with it any more."

Laban fixed his eyes on mine and I braced myself for a fight. Then, to my utter amazement, he backed down.

"All right," he shrugged. "Let's make a peace pact."

I was stunned. But before he could change his mind, I grabbed a large rock lying on the ground nearby and dragged it upright, and we all gathered up some smaller stones and heaped them into a mound in the dust. This was to mark the agreement between us.

"Let this rock and this heap of stones be a witness to our peace pact," Laban said. "I won't cross past them onto your side to hurt you and you mustn't cross them to my side to hurt me. And may God keep watch over us both."

The next morning, he kissed Rachel and Leah and his grandchildren goodbye, and set off for home. I was free of him at last.

My next big problem was Esau. The last time we'd seen each other he'd wanted me dead. And why not? I'd done him a terrible wrong. I knew I didn't deserve his forgiveness but, twenty years on, it's what I desperately wanted. Maybe sending men on ahead to let him know I was on my way was a better plan than barging in on him myself.

"Say to Esau that his servant, Jacob, has been staying with Laban and that he's coming home with plenty of livestock and a troop of servants," I told my messengers. "Say that he hopes we can be friends."

The messengers returned with the news that Esau was coming to meet me with four hundred of his men. That didn't sound like brotherly love to me.

I panicked. It wasn't just *my* life at stake any more. I had wives and children. If anything happened to them it would be my fault. I split us all up, people and animals, into two groups. If Esau attacked one, at least the other stood a chance of getting away. Then I turned to God. Finally, after all this time, I was coming to realise that all my planning was useless without Him. He was the only one who could help us now.

"Lord, you've been so good to me and I've done nothing to deserve it. You told me to go back to my home and my family, so here I am. Please help us. Protect us from my brother, Esau."

After I'd prayed, I felt calmer. I decided to send my servants on ahead of me again, but this time I let them go with a huge number of animals from my herds to give to Esau as a present. I told them to say that they were a gift to him from me and that I was following on behind. I hoped this might soften him up a bit before he actually saw me. As night fell,

we made camp, but it was still dark when I got everyone up and led them across a ford in the River Jabbok. Then I went back to get all our belongings brought over.

I happened to be on my own for a few moments when, out of the shadows, a man suddenly appeared. Before I could stop him, he hurled himself at me and began to wrestle with me there on the ground. He was strong but there was no way he was getting the better of me. And as we struggled together in the dust, somehow I knew he had come from God. I thought I was winning, but then the stranger freed one of his hands and managed to touch my hip. A searing pain shot through the joint. I thought he must have crippled me. Then, just as dawn began to send its pale glow along the horizon, he tried to get away.

"No," I snarled, grasping him with the little strength I had left. "You're not leaving until you give me God's blessing."

"What's your name?" the man asked.

"Jacob," I told him. I was surprised he didn't know.

"From now on your name will be Israel," the man answered, "because you've struggled with God and men but you've come through." Then he blessed me and was gone.

I was right about being crippled. After that night, I always limped when I walked.

However dazed and confused my weird encounter had left me,

it was nothing to the terrible fear that gripped me as I stood up and spotted my brother, Esau, striding towards us in the early morning light, with his four hundred men at his heels. This was it. There was no escape. Not any more. Was I a dead man?

"Jacob! Jacob, my brother!" Esau's cry rang in my ears, and suddenly his arms were around me and he hugged me and kissed me as though his life depended on it! I could hardly stand up as I gasped for breath and gazed into the tear-streaked face of the brother I had hurt so much, but who welcomed me now with such complete forgiveness.

"So, come on then," spluttered Esau at last, looking up at Rachel and Leah and the children huddled round them, "aren't you going to tell me where you found these?"
I couldn't help laughing, I was so relieved.
"These are my family," I told him, "my wives and our children."
Esau laughed too. "Well you've certainly been busy."
"You don't know the half of it," I said. "All the animals I sent on ahead are a present for you."
"Don't be daft," Esau murmured.
"No," I insisted, "take them, please. They're all yours. Seeing that look of love in your face after everything that's happened was like looking into the face of God."

And if ever God's face was looking down on me, I knew it was now.

LIONS, WHALES AND THRILLING TALES

Dear Samuel. . .

Ramah,
Nr. Jerusalem.

Dear Samuel,

Haven't you grown! When you came out to meet us the other week I thought, is that really my Samuel? I know I say the same thing every visit but it seems no time since you were just my little baby. And look at you now. I don't suppose those clothes I made will fit you for more than a couple of months. I'll have to get cracking on some more. But what a treat to be able to come and spend some time with you again. I wish it could be more often. Once a year just isn't enough.

Anyway, seeing you looking so grown up got me thinking that maybe this is a good time to write to you and explain just why we took you to live with that dear old priest, Eli, at Shiloh. I mean, you weren't even four years old when we left you with him, you couldn't possibly have understood. And I know we've talked about it lots of times since then, but I thought if I put it all in a letter, apart from anything else it

would set my mind at rest and let you know what a special boy you really are.

My first baby you were, something I thought I'd never have. Your dad had loads of children with his other wife, Penninah, but none with me. I knew how much he loved me but that couldn't make up for the emptiness I felt. Penninah was quite spiteful about it too. She used to tease me which I thought was horrid of her.

We started going to Shiloh once every year way before you were born. It's what a lot of people do. God chose to make it a holy place a long time ago, so we all travel there for a time of worship. But, of course, you know that now. Well, one year when we were there, Penninah started having a real go at me. I mean, it was bad enough being childless and having to see her surrounded by her kids every day, without having my nose rubbed in it as well. I got really upset and went off by myself to pray and let God know just how wretched I was feeling. I sobbed my heart out. I don't think I'd ever wanted Him to hear me as much as I did that night. I said to Him, "Lord, this is your servant, Hannah. I don't know what to do with this misery inside me. *Please* give me a son and I will give him back to you to serve you for the whole of his life."

I was so frantic in my prayer I felt all sort of breathless and the words came out in barely a whisper. Perhaps I had a bit of a wild look about me, I don't know, but Eli, who was still the priest back then, thought I'd been drinking and he told me as much. That didn't go down very well with me, as I'm sure you can imagine.

"I haven't been drinking," I said to him, "what do you take me for? I'm miserable, I've been crying to God." He was sorry then, I could see, and he asked God to give me peace and answer my prayers. And do you know, after that I felt calmer and happier than I had done for years.

We all went back home to Ramah next day and not long after that I found out I was pregnant with you! It was the most incredible thing. I can't even begin to tell you how it felt to have you growing inside me, moving around, kicking – and to know that God had listened to me. That's why I called you Samuel – because it sounds like our Hebrew word for "heard of God".

Mind you, it was a bit of a shock to the system becoming a mum and having my life turned upside down by this noisy little bundle who kept me up all night. I don't think anything can quite prepare you for it. Not that I'm complaining. I'd waited so long for a baby.

If giving birth to you was the best thing I've ever done, giving you up was certainly the hardest. But when I'd begged God for

a son, I'd also promised you to Him and I couldn't go back on
that. I told your dad we'd just wait until you were old enough
to manage without me. Then we'd take you to Shiloh to live
with the priest, Eli, and to learn how to serve God there.

When the time came, I thought I'd fall apart. How could I
let you go? But your dad's much more down to earth than I
am. Dear Elkanah, he's a great one for calling a spade and
spade. "You promised him to God, so to serve God he must
go," was what he said. And that was that.

But oh, Samuel, how it hurt to say goodbye. You were so
small, still little more than a baby really, and I knew it would
be a whole year till we next went back to Shiloh to offer our
worship to God and I could see you again. I took you to Eli
and said to him, "Do you remember me? I'm the woman
who begged God for a child, and this is the little boy He gave
me. Now I'm giving him back to God to serve Him here."
Good job your dad was there to buck me up.
"Stop your moping around, woman," he said to me. "You're
putting Samuel in God's hands. There's no safer place." I
know he was upset himself, but he wasn't going to let me see.

And he was right. You'd grow up with God. What better life
could you have?

Before we left you to come home to Ramah, I went off and

thanked God for what He'd done for me. I spent ages just pouring out what I felt. After all, even though I wouldn't be able to see very much of you, you'd always be my son. And do you know, God heard my heart again. He knew what a struggle it was for me to leave you, so one by one He gave me more babies to love and care for, brothers and sisters for you. Actually, I've a feeling there's another one on the way, but I haven't told your dad yet. I can hardly believe it sometimes when people ask, "How's the family?" That's *my* family they're talking about – the family I thought I'd never have.

So there you are, Samuel. You're a gift *from* God and a gift *for* God. He'll have a real purpose for you, you know. Just listen out for Him. He'll be there. And busy as I am – I mean, I'm rushed off my feet most days – there's not an hour goes by when I don't think of you. You'll always be my special boy.

I'd better finish now before I start getting all mushy and have your dad telling me to pull myself together. Take good care of yourself, child, and I can't wait to see you again next year.

God bless you.

With all my love always,

Mum xxxxxx

LIONS, WHALES AND THRILLING TALES

A Whale Of A Tale

THE BOOK OF JONAH

I could *not* believe it. There I was, a respected advisor in the very corridors of power at the court of King Jeroboam II, important people hanging on my every word. I loved God and the place where I lived. I was a happy man. So you can imagine how peeved I was when one day everything started to go more than a bit pear-shaped.

You see, I'm a prophet. God speaks to me and I tell others what He's said. I hadn't had a problem with it before. God had never said anything I didn't want to hear. But He did that day. He called to me, "Jonah." (That's my name – it means "dove".) "Jonah, I want you to travel abroad to a city called Nineveh and work with your enemies, the Assyrians. Tell them to stop doing wrong and to worship me."

I was stunned. Work with the Assyrians? Those people worshipped other gods. Anyway, Nineveh wasn't just round the corner. It was 700 miles away in Iraq. I wasn't some wild, round-the-world adventurer, why on earth would I want to go there? I didn't even like the Assyrians, and God was asking me to save them, to tell them that unless they turned from their bad ways within six weeks, the entire city of Nineveh would be destroyed.

Not likely, I thought, the Assyrians deserved everything God could throw at them. So if they didn't ask for forgiveness, they couldn't be forgiven. In other words no message from me, no escape for them. I didn't care if it *was* God speaking to me. I'd do anything He asked, but not that. So you know what I did? I went in the opposite direction. I packed my bags, bought my ticket and boarded a ship bound for Tarshish in the sunny south west of Spain. As far away as I could get.

It was a beautiful boat, with a rounded bow and a deck cover to protect us from bad weather, and there were great banks of oars down each side all ready for action should the wind die down. The voyage was delightful to start with. I even began to relax and to feel that, if nothing else, I deserved a good holiday. But I should have known it wouldn't last.

One morning when we were miles from land, the sky turned to a dusky pink and the birds stopped singing. An eerie stillness in the atmosphere made the hairs on the back of my neck stand on end. Then a wind sprang up, east-north-east I think the sailors said, and I watched uneasily as the waves started heaving.

"I suppose this is an occupational hazard," I shouted to one of the crew. Showers of salty spray were stinging my face like needles. The sailor didn't answer, just eyed the black banks of cloud building in the sky with the gathering storm.

"Best leave it to the experts then," I mumbled, and headed under cover to lie down. I can't say I was feeling too good and I must have fallen into a deep sleep. The next thing I knew the captain was shouting at me and shaking me awake. I could hardly hear him for the howling and crashing all around us. The storm had grown ferocious.

I scrambled back on deck, hanging on to anything that was nailed down to stop myself being thrown overboard. The terrified mariners were doing their best but even a complete land lubber like me could see it was hopeless. Those waves must have been six metres high and ready to swamp the ship as they broke over the bow. Typical, I found myself thinking, some dream cruise this is turning out to be. But as the wind whipped past, plastering my soaked hair across my face, I knew deep inside it was all my fault.

I felt the captain grip my arm.

"Please," he begged, his voice a desperate, rasping cry. "Please call on your God to save us!"

I gazed for a moment into his small, earnest eyes. The fear I saw there pierced me to my soul.

"I am a Hebrew man," I said, shouting close to the captain's

ear to make sure he heard every word. "I love God with all my heart but I'm disobeying Him. I'm running away. This storm is because of me!"

The captain stared at me as if he didn't believe a word, but I carried on.

"If you want to save yourselves, you'll have to throw me over the side into the sea."

"No," was the captain's unexpected response. "No, never!"

"It's the only way," I screamed back. He shook his head and before I could stop him had begun to haul himself to the other end of the ship to try to chart a new course towards land.

But this is God we're talking about. We were caught in a raging battle between sea and sailors. And the sailors were losing.

"I'm sorry!" came the captain's grief-stricken cry. He gave the order and his crew got ready to hurl me overboard. I heard him pleading to God for forgiveness. They were all convinced that would be the end of me. So was I. I wanted to scream out, "It's not your fault!" but it was too late. I hit the water and it closed over my head like the massive door to some enormous, freezing dungeon.

If God still had plans for me, apparently dying wasn't one of them. The instant my head disappeared the sea became as calm as a millpond, and I was left bobbing up and down like a cork. I was miserably cold and my tunic was rubbing. And then, get this, as if I hadn't been through enough already, I suddenly found myself nose to nose with an enormous fish. Seconds later it gulped me down! Its great gaping jaws closed around me and everything went black. All I could do was sit in the dark inside its stinking stomach, covered in rancid seaweed.

"Oh very clever, Jonah," I remember muttering to myself. "Running away from God, what a brilliant move that was."

Then I started to pray. I prayed like never before. After all, despite everything, God had saved me. He'd held on. All I could think of was to thank Him and promise that I would do what He wanted. I really meant it too.

It turned out to be a whole three days before this giant fish, spat me onto dry land with a massive burp! I mean, the indignity of it all. Fortunately there was no-one around to see.

That wasn't the end of it though, oh no. As I peeled off the seaweed God spoke to me again.
"Go to Nineveh and give the Assyrians my message."
I sighed. There was nothing for it. I'd have to obey God this time, but that didn't mean I was happy about it. The Assyrians were the arch-enemies of Israel and I had to offer them a chance to say sorry to God so that He could forgive them. I'm ashamed to say that deep down I hoped they wouldn't listen. I wanted them to be destroyed. I couldn't help it, I was hopping

mad, and as I trekked through Nineveh I must have preached my message with all the conviction of a wet weekend. But, would you believe it, the Assyrian people listened. Now I've seen God do some amazing things in my time but even I was absolutely flabbergasted.

Everyone in Nineveh, and we're talking 120,000 people give or take a few, took notice of what I said, turned away from their evil ways and believed in God. They felt so ashamed they even put on old sacks instead of their usual clothes to show how truly sorry they really were.

So, mission successful. You'd think by now I'd be a happy man. Well, you'd be wrong. I was grumpier than ever. Why was God being so kind? The Assyrians had turned their backs on Him to worship other gods, and they'd been sending nasty people into Israel to cause trouble.

I walked out of that city even more miserable than when I'd arrived. It just wasn't fair. And it was too hot. There were flies everywhere, I was sweating buckets. I needed to get out of the sun but there wasn't a patch of shade anywhere, not as far as the eye could see.

Then God stepped in again. As I stared miserably down at the dry, parched earth, the intense heat suddenly lessened, and the coolness of shadow began to dapple the ground all around me.

I glanced up, and towering overhead was a huge shrub. It seemed to grow out of nowhere and its broad leaves gave me enough precious shade to protect me from the sun's blazing rays. God must have planted it there. And it was beautiful.

You'll be pleased to hear that I cheered up a bit after that. As the sun went down I felt brighter than I had done for days, and in the cool of the evening was able to drift off to sleep. Perhaps, at long last, things were finally looking up.

But when I awoke the following morning, a hideous sight met my eyes. A worm, yes a miserable, beastly worm, had chewed right through the stem of my treasured plant and the entire shrub had withered and died. Then, to cap it all, a scorching east wind blew up and with the ferocity of the sun my head felt as if it would burst into flames. I'd never known anything like it. I was so dehydrated I thought I was done for. I even cried out to God, "It would be better for me to die than to live!"

How far was He trying to push me? Hadn't I been through enough? I'd been uprooted from my home, been sick as a dog on my cruise to Spain, I'd been thrown overboard, swallowed by a fish, I'd helped to save thousands of evil people who should have got what was coming to them, my gorgeous plant had been eaten by a worm, and now the rays of the sun had burnt the top of my head. I was fuming! I felt I'd bottled it all up pretty well until now, but this time I'd had enough.

"Why are you doing this?" I shook my fists and exploded with rage at God. "What is it you want from me?"

God's voice broke through my fury.
"Why are you so upset about this plant?" He said. "Is it yours? Did you look after it, water it, help it grow? You did nothing for it and yet you really care that it's gone. Can't you understand how much I care about the thousands of people in Nineveh who I love with all my heart, but whose lives are a complete mess because they know next to nothing about me?"

I forgot the heat. Suddenly I did understand. God was right. I was more concerned about a tree than about the lives of the Assyrian people who didn't love Him. I'd tried to turn my back on them. I'd even wished for them to have a taste of their own bitter medicine. It was a hard lesson but God's a good teacher. He showed me that I should pray for my enemies, not hate them for the things they do. I should learn to love them just as God loves me.

And God does love me. He's good to me too. There can't be many men who've been swallowed by a fish and lived to tell the tale.

A Whale Of A Tale

Lions, Whales And Thrilling Tales

Esther, The Surprising Queen

THE BOOK OF ESTHER, CHAPTERS 1–3

Talk about hot gossip! When Queen Vashti was banished for refusing to obey an order from her husband, King Xerxes of Persia, everyone was talking about it – not so much because she was sent away, but because she had the nerve to say no.

You see, King Xerxes (pronounced Zerk-sees) was very rich and powerful. He ruled over one hundred and twenty-seven provinces stretching from India to northern Sudan, so I suppose he did have a lot to show off about. When he'd been king for three years, he organised a huge festival that went on for six whole months to let people know just how great he really was. To round it all off, he gave an enormous banquet for the men living in the capital city of Susa where he reigned. It lasted for seven days. King Xerxes certainly wasn't a man to do things by halves, and as his queen was known for her incredible beauty, he wanted to show her off as well. So he ordered her to come and meet his guests. But Queen Vashti had other ideas. She was busy entertaining all the women of Susa with a party of her own, and it must have been more than a bit embarrassing for the king when she refused to show up.

King Xerxes went mad and sent for his advisors. They told him the queen would have to go, otherwise women everywhere would hear how she had disobeyed him, and think they had the right to disobey their husbands too. "If you don't make a stand," they said, "there'll be chaos."

So that was the last anyone ever saw of Queen Vashti. Then the king sent letters all over his empire giving orders that every husband must be head of his household and stand no nonsense. No woman was going to make an idiot out of *him*.

There was a war in Greece not long after that, so I suppose King Xerxes had a lot on his mind. It was another four years before he got round to thinking about finding a new queen. This is where I come in. I'm Esther. At least, I'm Esther now. My parents called me Hadassah, but my name got changed when my family and I and a lot of others were taken prisoner by Nebuchadnezzar, the King of Babylon. That's how we came to Susa in the first place. We were brought here from Jerusalem. Anyway, I prefer the name Esther. It's easier to spell. And when the king's search for a queen began, I was one of the girls brought to live in his harem for him to choose from. The harem was an apartment at the palace that was strictly women only – except for a few special members of staff whose job it was to look after us.

I suppose it was quite flattering to end up there at all. Queen

Vashti's looks were obviously a lot to live up to, so the king
was only interested in meeting beautiful girls. But we all
must have fallen short of the mark. Before we were even
allowed to *see* the king, we had to go through intensive
beauty therapy – and I'm not just talking a week or two. I
can still remember the shock wave that ran round the room
when Hegai, who was in charge of us, announced, "This is
the beginning of a twelve-month beauty programme."

Twelve months! Was it really going to take that long to get us
up to scratch?
"During the year," he continued, "you will be introduced to the
benefits of a wide range of exotic oils, perfumes and cosmetics,
not forgetting, of course, a very special diet to assist in drawing
out your inner beauty."
That's how Hegai talked all the time. He was very posh, but
quite sweet. I don't know why but he seemed to take to me
more than to the others. He even arranged for seven maids
from the palace to come and look after me and gave us the best
accommodation in the harem. It was all a bit unreal. I mean, if
you'd told me a month before that I'd soon be being pampered
to pieces as a guest of King Xerxes, I'd have laughed.

A year did seem a long time though. A lot of the girls were
really homesick. It wasn't so bad for me because I was already
living in Susa with my father, Mordecai. Mordecai wasn't my
real father. He was actually my cousin but he adopted me

when both my parents died. I missed him, especially at the beginning. That whole twelve months, he used to come and wait outside the palace every day to find out how I was getting on. He said not to tell anyone he was my step dad. He seemed to think it best if no-one knew anything about my family. But he'd be there if I needed him.

So, there we were, all girls together. As time went on we got really friendly. It didn't seem to matter which one of us got King Xerxes in the end. The day when we'd actually meet him seemed too far off for it to be important.

It came round though.
"You'll be introduced one at a time," Hegai told us, "and when you've had your meeting we shan't see you again here. You'll be taken back to another part of the harem."
What a shame! That meant no sneak previews of what the king was like before it was my turn. Of course I'd seen him before, but actually being in the same room with him, face to face, eyeball to eyeball, sharing the same bit of air space, what would that be like? I tried to think of all the common sense stuff – smile, sit up straight, agree with everything he says, don't pick your nose, but most of all, LOOK INTERESTED. King Xerxes was hardly going to look twice at anyone stifling a yawn.

When I did find myself standing in front of him, it was

nothing like I thought it would be. Actually, I felt sick. I had to keep thinking, "Oh well, it'll all be over soon. Then I'll be able to join the others and we can have a good gossip and swap notes."

But I was a bit ahead of myself. You see, I was the one the king did look at twice. I was the one he chose. It was me he crowned queen.

It took a bit of getting used to, my new life. I was so glad Mordecai was around. He never came into the palace. He still felt I shouldn't tell anyone who he was, but he'd come and sit at the gate. And just knowing he was there, hovering in the background, somehow made all the difference.

In the end it made a huge difference to King Xerxes too.

One day when Mordecai was taking his usual stroll near the palace, he happened to overhear the two gatekeepers whispering together, and of all things, they were hatching a plot to kill the king! Mordecai told me at once and I was able to let King Xerxes know. There was a big investigation, the gatekeepers were found guilty and they were hanged on the spot.
"It's no thanks to me," I made sure the king understood. "It's Mordecai you should be grateful to."

And he was. He even had the whole thing written up in the court diary.

For quite a while after that, I just got on with being queen. I enjoyed it really and the next four years shot by. Of course, there were court rules, but I got to know them pretty quickly. One thing I was told I must *never* do was go and see the king without an invitation when he was in his private chambers. There was a death penalty for that. I thought it was a bit over the top, but I didn't say anything. Only a half-wit would challenge the king's laws. Anyway, I wanted to be a good queen and I think I was probably doing all right. It was this man called Haman who nearly spoilt everything.

Haman and King Xerxes had become best buddies, and the king decided to give him the most important job in the palace. I don't know why, Haman was a real show-off. He got even worse when the king ordered everyone to show him special respect by bowing down to him. I'm surprised he could still get his head through the palace gate. Naturally everyone obeyed, they wouldn't dare not to. At least I assumed everyone obeyed. But it turned out there was one man who refused – and of all people, it was my step dad, Mordecai.

You see, Mordecai was a Jew. Our whole family were Jews, but no-one at the palace knew that about me. That's why

Mordecai was being disobedient. He loved God. He couldn't kneel down to Haman because only God deserves worship like that.

It was my maids who told me what a state Mordecai was in. They said he'd stopped eating, and was seen crying all the time. He'd even taken off his proper clothes and wrapped himself up in old sacking. You only did that if something really terrible was going on. But Mordecai had always been so strong, he could cope with anything. I could feel the panic rising in my chest. I called for Hathach, one of my servants. "Find out," I said to him, "find out what's wrong. If something bad's happened I need to know."

Hathach bowed and left. For the first time since my wedding, the palace suddenly seemed very empty. It was as if Mordecai was lost somewhere. And all I could do was wait.

The Great Escape

THE BOOK OF ESTHER, CHAPTERS 3–10

I wasn't very good at waiting for Hathach to return with
news of Mordecai. I couldn't sit still and I certainly couldn't
think straight. He'd been gone for ages. What could be
taking so long?

When he finally reappeared, he looked awful. I rushed
straight up to him, searching his eyes for some reassurance.
There was none, just a deep sadness.
"Well?" I demanded.
Hathach hung his head and said quietly, "I'm afraid it's not
good news."

He told me that when the palace gate staff realised Mordecai
was going against the king's command, they reported him to
Haman. Haman was absolutely furious and, to get his own
back, he planned to have Mordecai killed, and then to
murder every single Jew living in the king's empire. He
wanted to wipe out the lot of us. So he got together with his
cronies, who were a superstitious bunch, and they'd thrown
dice or something to pick a day when all these terrible
killings should happen. Thankfully for all of us the date was a

good way off, about eleven months, but Haman still went right to the king to get everything sorted early. He made it sound as if all Jews were disobedient and evil. He said that, for the sake of his majesty, they should be got rid of, every single one. He also promised to put something like £3,000,000 into the royal treasury as payment for the killings, money which would all be taken from the Jewish people. And King Xerxes, who had no idea *I* was Jew, was going along with it!

Haman had already had letters written in the king's name commanding all Jews to be found and killed on the chosen day, and their land and possessions taken. The letters were sealed with the royal seal, then sent out to every province in the empire.

So that was Haman's grisly little plot. I felt sick to my stomach. No-one escaped the king's law. What could I do? There was nothing, not now the royal seal was on everything. My mind was racing. I was only vaguely aware that Hathach was still standing there.

"What is it?" I murmured. What more could there possibly be?

"I have a request for you from Mordecai," Hathach answered hesitantly. "He wants you to go to the king and ask him to spare the lives of the Jews."

I stared at him. It wasn't cold but I was shivering.

"I can't," I heard myself saying. "Hathach, you know I can't. The king hasn't asked for me in a month. If I go and see him without being invited, he'll have me killed."

"I know," Hathach nodded. "I'll go back to Mordecai and make sure he understands."

But I should have known Mordecai wouldn't leave it there. I'd never been able to say no to him in my life!

Back came his answer.

"Just because you live in the palace doesn't mean you'll escape." I could picture his face as he spoke, the earnest expression in his sad, dark eyes.

"You're a Jew," his message went on. "Haman's death sentence is for you too. You're the only one of us who can talk to King Xerxes. Don't you understand? The very reason God gave you the queen's crown may have been for such a time as this."

It was a lot to get my head round. But if Mordecai was right, then I had no choice. I couldn't ignore God. I had to find a way of saving the Jews. Anyway, how could I turn my back on my own people?

I needed a plan.

"Tell Mordecai to get together with all the Jews in Susa," I said to Hathach, "and hold a fast for me for three days and nights. Don't eat or drink anything. Pray instead. I'll do the same here with my maids. Then God will know we desperately need His help. After that, I'll go and see the king."

When I saw the alarm flash across Hathach's face, all I could do was shrug and try to smile.

"If it means I must die... then I must die," I murmured. But I sounded a lot braver than I felt.

Even without food, those three days went horribly quickly, and as I got ready to face King Xerxes, I felt faint and dizzy. Still, I had to keep to my plan. I'd worked out exactly what to say and how to say it... but would I get the chance?

I stood outside the king's private chamber. The door was open but I stayed in the shadows to one side so he couldn't see me. It was a miracle he didn't hear my heart thudding. And Mordecai's words kept flashing through my mind – for such a time as this. I had to make my move before I fainted. So I closed my eyes, and knowing I had to be braver than I'd ever been in my whole life, I stepped into the doorway.

King Xerxes was sitting on his royal throne facing me. For a moment, he didn't seem to notice I was there. Then his eyes flicked towards me. I froze. I could see his golden sceptre, the special royal staff, lying in his lap. The custom was that if he picked it up and held it out to an uninvited visitor, it meant the visitor was safe and could approach him. But if he just let

it lie, then that visitor was as good as dead.

I don't know how long I stood there. I could hardly breathe
let alone move. I didn't even notice King Xerxes pick up the
sceptre, but suddenly there it was, stretched out towards me,
glinting as it caught the light. It was all right! The king was
smiling. He wasn't angry or offended, he wasn't going to have
me killed. The faintness swept over me again. As I took a step
towards him, I was afraid if I didn't concentrate I'd fall flat
on my face.

"What is it, my queen?" I heard him say. "What do you want
to ask me? You know I will give you up to half my kingdom."
But would he give me the lives of the Jews? In spite of his
good mood, I knew better than to ask him on the spot, so I
kept to my plan and invited him and Haman to dinner that
day. How I got the words out, I'll never know.

King Xerxes seemed pleased to be asked, and they both
arrived right on time. The servants put on a wonderful
spread. Haman was his usual creepy self, but I didn't expect
anything different. When we'd finished eating, King Xerxes
leaned back in his chair and looked at me thoughtfully.
"Come on, then," he said. "What is it Queen Esther wants
me to do for her?"
If only you knew, I thought as I smiled back at him.
"Come to dinner again tomorrow," I answered. "Bring

Haman. Then I'll tell you."

Of course, Haman was even more unbearable after that. One of my maids overheard him boasting his head off about how rich he was, and how the king thought more highly of him than of anyone else in the royal court. Now he could brag that he was the only person I'd invited to a private dinner with King Xerxes – and not just once, but twice.

Mordecai was still getting to him, though. In fact the more full of himself Haman was, the more it annoyed him that Mordecai was so obviously unimpressed.

After the success of my dinner party, I could hardly believe it when the following day began so badly. In the morning I was told that, under Haman's orders, some gallows were being built in the city. They were to be huge, about twenty-five metres high. Haman had decided to get the king's permission to hang Mordecai before they both came to eat with me that evening. He wanted him off his mind for good.

There was nothing for it. I'd have to scrap my plan, take a huge risk and go and see King Xerxes again. But as I was getting ready, one of my maids brought me the best news. She said the king hadn't been able to sleep the night before and, to pass the time, he'd ordered the court diary to be brought in and read out to him. When it came to the part where Mordecai had uncovered the plot to kill him five years before, King Xerxes remembered that he had never given Mordecai any special honours as a thank you. And who had he asked how he should honour Mordecai but Haman! Only, being such a big head, Haman misunderstood and thought the king was wanting to honour *him*. So of course he came up with something really flashy. He said the chosen man should be given one of the king's robes to wear, one of the king's horses to ride on, and should then be led through the streets of Susa by the most trusted of the king's staff.

"I love it!" cried King Xerxes. "Go and do everything you've said for Mordecai, and you be the one to lead him on my horse."

How I wish I could have seen Haman's face! There he was about to ask for permission to hang Mordecai, and now he had orders to give him the highest possible honours from the king. The timing was perfect. Only God could have arranged it like that.

Haman was a lot quieter at our second dinner that evening, but King Xerxes didn't seem to notice. He had other things on his mind. He was very curious to know what I was going to ask him.

The moment came. He repeated his question from the day before. What was it I wanted him to do for me? I hesitated.

With Haman sitting there, it was much harder to ask than I thought it would be.

"I want you to spare my life, your majesty, and the lives of all my people who have been condemned to death."

There. I'd said it. Haman went pale. He looked like a ghost, staring at me with hollow, disbelieving eyes. I was a Jew and all this time he hadn't a clue.

King Xerxes was so angry he could scarcely speak. In a low, barely controlled voice he asked, "Who has dared order this?"

"Haman." I spoke the name and looked away. The king leapt up from the table, knocking his wine to the floor. Then he stormed outside.

I couldn't move and I couldn't look at Haman.

"Please," I heard him whisper. "I didn't know you were a Jew. If I had, I never would have given the order."

I had nothing to say.

"I'm begging you," he went on, "please, don't let the king take my life."

Then, before I could stop him, he suddenly threw himself at my feet. But that was another mistake. When the king came back in, he thought Haman was attacking me. I suppose any idea he may have had of sparing his life vanished at that

point. He ordered Haman to be hung – on the very gallows Haman had had built for Mordecai.

That should have been the end of it, but it wasn't. The problem was that once an order was written in the king's name, it couldn't be cancelled. It had to be carried out. I was devastated. After everything I'd done it looked as if we were all going to die anyway. But then King Xerxes had a brilliant idea. "We'll send out another order," he said to me, "and we'll seal it with the royal seal. We'll make it law that when the day comes for the Jews to be attacked, they now have the right to defend themselves."

Scary as the king was if you upset him, if you kept in his good books, it certainly paid off. Orders were sent out across his huge empire, and although the Jews did have to fight for their lives, in the end we were saved – a whole nation.

Mordecai was given Haman's old job of prime minister in the palace, and because we'd all had such an amazing escape, he wanted Jews throughout the kingdom to remember what had happened by holding a celebration. That's where the festival of Purim comes from. Every year on the thirteenth day of the month we call Adar, which was the day Haman picked for the murder of the Jews, Jewish people hold a fast to remember how God helped them to save themselves. The fourteenth and fifteenth days of the month are for feasting and giving presents.

Mordecai is very popular here because of all the good work
he does and the way he looks after his people, and as there's
no need to keep my Jewish roots a secret any more, I make
sure everyone knows he's my dad. He's the brains and I'm the
heart of the palace. We might have died with all the other
Jews, but God saved us. The good guys won in the end.

The Death Cheaters

THE BOOK OF DANIEL, CHAPTERS 1–6

"There's another one. Grab him!"

I tried to run but it was no good. A heavy hand clamped itself round my arm and a soldier stuck his sweaty, bristly chin in my face.

"What's your name?" he snarled.

"Daniel," I gasped.

"Right then, Daniel. Don't struggle and you won't get hurt."

He hauled me into the street. Jerusalem was in uproar. People were running and screaming. The whole place was crawling with soldiers. King Nebuchadnezzar of Babylon was taking over our city. Jehoiakim, King of Judah, was his prisoner. And I was being kidnapped!

It wasn't just me. A huge crowd of us were dragged out of our homes in Jerusalem and bundled off to Babylon. I hardly dared think what might happen when we got there. We were all terrified. But, actually, it wasn't so bad.

We'd only been there a short time when a group of us were

picked to be trained up to serve in King Nebuchadnezzar's palace.

"The King is after young men from the best family backgrounds," Ashpenaz, the chief court official, announced one day. "He wants the clever ones, but you've got to be good-looking as well."

We were put into training for three years and taught all we needed to know about the language and people of Babylon. The king even sent us food and wine from his own table to make sure we kept strong and healthy. But it was tricky. I didn't want to eat the king's food. I wasn't being awkward it's just that God had made rules about what His people could eat, and King Nebuchadnezzar's food went against them. Because I loved God, I didn't want to let Him down. Three of my friends felt the same, so I asked Ashpenaz for permission to eat something different but he was too afraid of the king to go against him.

"If King Nebuchadnezzar sees you getting pale and thin because I've disobeyed him," Ashpenaz said, "he'll have me executed."

So I went to the guard in charge of us.

"Just give us vegetables and water," I said to him. "Then see how we are after ten days."

Reluctantly he agreed, but God made sure we looked healthier than any of the trainees who were eating the king's food. The guard was mystified.

"Beats me how you look so good just on veggies," he muttered, but he let us carry on.

We finally finished our training and were presented to King Nebuchadnezzar. I never really thought that, out of all the men picked for training, we'd be the ones chosen to serve the king in his palace. But we were. The king settled on me and my three friends.

Some time after our appointment to the court, King Nebuchadnezzar started having nightmares. They upset him enough to send for some of his wise men, but he didn't just want to know what the nightmares meant. He wanted these men to describe what had happened in the dream. Perhaps he'd forgotten, I don't know, but they couldn't tell him a thing. They needed to know what the dream was before they could even begin to explain it.

The king was so furious because they couldn't do what he asked that he sentenced all the wise men in Babylon to death. Including me! I had to think quickly. Only God could do what King Nebuchadnezzar asked, so I went to the king and asked for more time. I knew if I caught him in a really bad mood, he'd probably have me executed on the spot. Thankfully he agreed and I shot off to find my friends.

"We must beg God to save us," I urged them. "He's the only

one who can tell us this dream and its meaning."
I don't think we'd ever prayed so hard in our lives. God
didn't let us down. That night he showed me what we needed
to know. When I went back to the king, he could hardly
believe his ears.

I described the massive statue he had seen in his dream and
how it was shattered by a blow from a single rock. The rock
then grew into a vast mountain which spread out and
covered the whole world.
"God is showing you the future," I explained. "When the
empire of Babylon comes to an end, three more great empires
will follow, one after the other. When the last is up and
running, God will create a fifth kingdom. This one will last
forever."

Before I could stop him, King Nebuchadnezzar had thrown
himself on the ground in front of me.
"Your God is truly the God of Gods," he murmured. "How
else could He reveal something so incredible?"
Then he gave me an instant promotion. He put me in charge
of the whole province of Babylon and, at my request,
appointed my three friends, Shadrach, Meshach and
Abednego as administrators.

The next few years were good for all four of us. Then one day
things went badly wrong.

Forgetting about God, King Nebuchadnezzar built a massive gold statue to represent one of his own gods. It was gigantic at ninety feet high and nine feet wide. All the important officials from the kingdom of Babylon were invited to the grand opening. Fortunately I was able to stay at the palace, but Shadrach, Meshach and Abednego went along. They were horrified, especially when the king's herald announced that everyone must bow down and worship the statue as soon as the musicians started to play.

"How can we do that to God?" Abednego said. "How can we let Him down?"

Well, of course, they didn't. But the king, who was pretty hot-tempered, had threatened anyone who refused to obey the command with instant death by roasting alive in a furnace. When he heard of my friends' disobedience, he was beside himself with fury.

"Throw us in the furnace if you wish, Your Majesty," they said to him. "God has the power to save us from fire if He wants. But even if He decides not to, we can't turn our backs on Him and bow down to your statue."

King Nebuchadnezzar flew into an uncontrollable rage. "Stoke up the furnace!" he bellowed. "Make it seven times hotter than usual!"

Then the guards came. Shadrach, Meshach and Abednego

were tied up and thrown into the fire. The heat was so intense that it killed the guards, but it didn't even touch my friends. "We should have been burned to a frazzle," Shadrach told me. "But God was right there. He sent an angel to protect us."

They all said that the best part was looking through the furnace door and seeing the look of utter amazement on King Nebuchadnezzar's face. He just couldn't believe his eyes, and when he called them out, there wasn't a trace of a singe mark. They didn't even smell smoky.

Once again King Nebuchadnezzar was forced to recognise God's greatness.
"No other god could do what yours has done," he murmured, "and you were prepared to die for Him. From now on, no-one shall say anything against Him – on pain of death."

God had to remind King Nebuchadnezzar for a third time of His great power, and before he died, the king finally did come to worship Him with his whole heart.

Many years later, when Belshazzar was King of Babylon, I found myself having to deliver some very bad news. King Belshazzar had invited one thousand of his noblemen to a banquet. They were all drinking wine together when the king suddenly commanded his servants to bring in the gold and silver cups that Nebuchadnezzar had stolen from God's temple in Jerusalem years ago when I was kidnapped. Then he and his guests used them to drink toasts to their own gods. But their gods weren't real. They were just statues. What an insult to our living God! And what a laugh they all had over it. But not for long.

Suddenly, out of nowhere, a human hand appeared. With an outstretched finger it began to write on the palace wall. The scoffing and cackling sank to a horrified silence, and the king, by all accounts, turned so white he looked transparent. "Send for my wise men," he spluttered. "Fetch them now. If any one of them can explain this writing to me, I will give them great power throughout my kingdom."

The wise men arrived. They peered at the writing on the wall and they scratched their heads, but not one of them could give King Belshazzar the faintest clue as to what it meant.

It was the queen mother who remembered me and how, with God's help, I'd been able to tell King Nebuchadnezzar his dream.
"Get Daniel," she commanded. "He'll know."
I was summoned. King Belshazzar promised me wealth and power in return for an explanation of the words on the wall, but I didn't want his presents. As I gazed at the writing, I could hardly bring myself to look at him.

"God gave great knowledge and power to your ancestor, Nebuchadnezzar," I began. "But when he got too full of himself, it was all taken away until he turned to God again and recognised Him as the living Lord of all. You knew this, but you still turned your back on God. You used the precious cups that belong to His temple to drink to your own man-made gods. Well, now God has had enough. He sent the hand you saw and what is written is this:

You are not the king you should be. Your reign is over and the kingdom that was yours will be handed over to the people of Media and Persia."

That was all. And that night King Belshazzar was murdered. The Medes and the Persians took over Babylon and Darius became the new king.

King Darius immediately appointed one hundred and twenty ministers to run his kingdom, and three administrators (I was one of them) to be in overall charge. I was an old man by then, but King Darius obviously trusted me and I worked hard for him. I thanked God over and over for the way things had worked out for me. Three times a day I knelt by my upstairs window, which faced towards my old home town of Jerusalem, and I prayed.

Perhaps the other officials got jealous because Darius

thought so highly of me, but they hated me enough to hatch
a plot to get rid of me. Because they couldn't find anything
wrong with the way I was doing my job, they used God
against me. They went to King Darius and encouraged him
to pass a law that anyone found praying to any god in the
next thirty days would be thrown to the lions. By the time I
heard of this ridiculous order, the king had put his signature
to it and, as with all the laws of the Medes and the Persians,
once it was in writing, it couldn't be changed.

If I obeyed the law and stopped praying for a month, it
meant I was putting the king's wishes before God. As I'd
never put anything before God in my whole life, I certainly
wasn't going to start now. I suppose I could have prayed in
secret, but what for? God is my God forever, why hide it? So
I carried on as before, three times a day, kneeling at my open
window. Of course, the officials were thrilled to bits. I'd
played right into their hands, and they lost no time running
to the king to tell tales. King Darius was very upset. He
didn't want to lose me, but try as he might, he couldn't find a
way to save me. The law had to stand.

It was late. Suddenly there was a loud banging on my door.
"Open up, Daniel, you're under arrest!"
A damp, cold sweat crept across my forehead. My spine
prickled. I opened the door slowly and stepped outside.
Several large, hairy-looking guards were standing in the dark

waiting for me.

"Here he is, lads," growled one of them. He smiled at me nastily as he grasped my arm.

"All ready to go are we, Daniel? You've got an appointment with some lions. Yum, yum."

They needn't have been so rough. I was frightened, yes, I was terrified, but I wasn't going to run. God had been with me all these years, and whatever happened, I knew He wouldn't leave me now.

"May your God save you!" cried King Darius. Those were the last words I heard. One shove from the guard and I lay sprawled full length on the dirty ground in the lions' pit. The sharp acid smell stung my nostrils.

For a while I daredn't move. I had a silly idea that if I lay completely still, the lions might not see me. They did though. There was hot breath on the back of my neck. Bristling whiskers brushed against my head. I wanted to be sick. Any minute now...

But nothing happened. The lion moved away. Slowly, very slowly, I lifted my head. I was surrounded by the huge, shaggy-headed beasts, but far from being poised, ready to spring, they just gazed at me disinterestedly. It wasn't until I sat up that I realised I wasn't alone. There was someone else in the pit.

At first light I heard King Darius call down, "Daniel. Daniel, are you still alive?"

"I am, Your Majesty," I answered softly. "God saved me. He knew I'd done nothing wrong so He sent an angel to protect me."

"Get him out! Get him out now!" King Darius yelled at his guards, and they hoisted me up. The men who had spoken against me were hurled into the pit instead. And the lions tore them limb from limb.

King Darius was so flabbergasted to see me without even a scratch, that he passed a new law ordering everyone throughout the land for evermore to fear and worship my God. I was thrilled. You see, my God is for everyone, the living Lord who saved me from the lions' jaws.

CanaanPress

The Lying Tree
ISBN: 978-0-9551816-3-4
RRP £6.99

Available now at
www.canaanpress.co.uk

Also by Alexa Tewkesbury and Steve Legg

Jamie Bryce is a lonely, eleven-year-old boy whose mum has walked out on him. When he and his dad move away to start a new life without her, Jamie decides no one's ever going to know the truth. It'll be easy. He'll never tell anyone anything about himself – especially not that his mum didn't love him enough to stay. If someone asks, he can make it all up. He can be whoever he wants to be, invent an entire life.

But keeping up with all his lies doesn't turn out to be that simple. And after a curious meeting with a stranger one day after school, things take a decidedly sinister turn...

Written by the award-winning creators of *It's A Boy!*, *The Lying Tree* is the gripping story of what happened when a young boy's lies became his life.